THE
PRISON-INDUSTRIAL
COMPLEX

&THE GLOBAL
ECONOMY

PMPRESS

PM Press PAMPHLET SERIES

0001: BECOMING THE MEDIA: A CRITICAL HISTORY OF CLAMOR MAGAZINE
By Jen Angel

0002: DARING TO STRUGGLE, FAILING TO WIN: THE RED ARMY FACTION'S 1977 CAMPAIGN OF DESPERATION
By J. Smith And André Moncourt

0003: MOVE INTO THE LIGHT: POSTSCRIPT TO A TURBULENT 2007
By The Turbulence Collective

0004: THE PRISON-INDUSTRIAL COMPLEX AND THE GLOBAL ECONOMY
By Eve Goldberg and Linda Evans

0005: ABOLISH RESTAURANTS
By Prole

0006: SING FOR YOUR SUPPER: A DIY GUIDE TO PLAYING MUSIC, WRITING SONGS, AND BOOKING YOUR OWN GIGS
By David Rovics

0007: PRISON ROUND TRIP
By Klaus Viehmann

PM Press Pamphlet Series No. 0004

The Prison-Industrial Complex and the Global Economy
By Eve Goldberg and Linda Evans

ISBN: 978-1-60486-043-6

Originally published in 1998 by Agit Press

PM Press
Po Box 23912
Oakland, CA 94623
www.pmpress.org

Layout and Design: Daniel Meltzer

Printed in Oakland, CA on recycled paper with soy ink.

TABLE OF CONTENTS

STATISTICS

The following updated prison information and statistics taken from a 12/07 justice department report were provided by BO (r.d. brown).

The u.s. prison population's explosion is an ever growing cancer: 7 MILLION people—one in every 32 adults—are behind bars. Of those, 2.2 million are in jail; more than 4.1 million are on probation; and almost 1 million are on parole.

The rate of imprisonment for women continues to grow at a faster pace than for males; though the women are still less than 3% of the total. Misguided (or perhaps purposeful) policies that create harsher sentences for non-violent drug crimes are responsible for this ridiculous rise. From 1995–2003 prisoner population in federal prisons increased by 49%. Racial disparity (phrase of the new language for racism) also continues. In the 25–29 age group, close to 9% or 1 in 13 Black men are prisoners; compared with 2.6% Latino/Hispanic men and 1.1% for white men. Black women are twice as likely as Latinas and three times as likely as white women to be in prison. Therefore, the information in these few pages should be required reading for everyone. The importance of understanding the P.I.C. is learning how not to run a country, and we must know this in order to create a different world for the planet and for ourselves. History does not have to repeat itself. We must begin today to think differently and to certainly act differently or we will continue to destroy our tomorrow.

GOING INTO THE PRISON

by Chrystos

the guard growls, What's this?!
Poetry, I answer, just Poetry
He waves me through
with a yawn
that delights me
So I smuggle my words in
to the women
who bite them chewing starving
I'm honored to serve them
bring color   music   feelings
into that soul death
Smiling as I weep
for Poetry who has such a bad reputation
She's boring, unnecessary, incomprehensible
obscure, effete
The perfect weapon
for this sneaky old war horse
to make a rich repast of revolution

for Linda Evans

PRISONS ARE BIG BUSINESS

Like the military/industrial complex, the prison-industrial complex is an interweaving of private business and government interests. Its two-fold purpose is profit and social control. Its public rationale is the fight against crime.

Not so long ago, communism was "the enemy" and communists were demonized as a way of justifying gargantuan military expenditures. Now, fear of crime and the demonization of criminals serve a similar ideological purpose: to justify the use of tax dollars for the repression and incarceration of a growing percentage of our population. The omnipresent media blitz about serial killers, missing children, and "random violence" feeds our fear. In reality, however, most of the "criminals" we lock up are poor people who commit nonviolent crimes out of economic need. Violence occurs in less than 14% of all reported crime, and injuries occur in just 3%. In California, the top three charges for those entering prison are: possession of a controlled substance, possession of a controlled substance for sale, and robbery. Violent crimes like murder, rape, manslaughter and kidnapping don't even make the top ten.

Like fear of communism during the Cold War, fear of crime is a great selling tool for a dubious product.

As with the building and maintenance of weapons and armies, the building and maintenance of prisons are big business. Investment houses, construction companies, architects, and support services such as food, medical, transportation and furniture, all stand to profit by prison expansion. A burgeoning "specialty item" industry sells fencing, handcuffs, drug detectors, protective vests, and other security devices to prisons.

As the Cold War winds down and the Crime War heats up, defense industry giants like Westinghouse are re-tooling and lobbying Washington for their share of the domestic law enforcement market. "Night Enforcer" goggles used in the Gulf War, electronic "Hot Wire" fencing ("so hot NATO chose it for high-risk installations"), and other equipment once used by the military, are now being marketed to the criminal justice system.

Communication companies like AT&T, Sprint, and MCI are getting into the act as well, gouging prisoners with exorbitant phone calling rates, often six times the normal long distance charge. Smaller firms like Correctional Communications Corp., dedicated solely to the prison phone business, provide computerized prison phone systems, fully equipped for systematic surveillance. They win government contracts by offering to "kick back" some of the profits to the government agency awarding the contract. These companies are reaping huge profits at the expense of prisoners and their families; prisoners are often effectively cut off from communication due to the excessive cost of phone calls.

One of the fastest growing sectors of the prison-industrial complex is private corrections companies. Investment firm Smith Barney is a part owner of a prison in Florida. American Express and General Electric have invested in private prison construction in Oklahoma and Tennessee. Correctional Corporation Of America, one of the largest private prison owners, already operates internationally, with more than 48 facilities in 11 states, Puerto Rico, the United Kingdom, and Australia. Under contract by government to run jails and prisons, and paid a fixed sum per prisoner, the profit motive mandates that these firms operate as cheaply and efficiently as possible. This means lower wages for staff, no unions, and fewer services for prisoners. Private contracts also mean less public scrutiny. Prison owners are raking in billions by cutting corners which harm prisoners. Substandard diets, extreme overcrowding, and abuses by poorly trained personnel have all been documented and can be expected in these institutions which are unabashedly about making money.

Prisons are also a leading rural growth industry. With traditional agriculture being pushed aside by agribusiness, many rural American communities are facing hard times. Economically depressed areas are falling over each other to secure a prison facility of their own. Prisons are seen as a source of jobs—in construction, local vendors and prison staff—as well as a source of tax revenues. An average prison has a staff of several hundred employees and an annual payroll of several million dollars.

Like any industry, the prison economy needs raw materials. In this case the raw materials are prisoners. The prison-industrial complex can grow only if more and more people are incarcerated—even if crime rates drop. "Three Strikes" and mandatory minimums (harsh, fixed sentences without parole) are two examples of the legal superstructure quickly being put in place to guarantee that the prison population will grow and grow and grow.

LABOR & THE FLIGHT OF CAPITAL

The growth of the prison-industrial complex is inextricably tied to the fortunes of labor. Ever since the onset of the Reagan-Bush years in 1980, workers in the United States have been under siege. Aggressive union busting, corporate deregulation, and especially the flight of capital in search of cheaper labor markets, have been crucial factors in the downward plight of American workers.

One wave of capital flight occurred in the 1970s. Manufacturing such as textiles in the Northeast moved south—to South Carolina, Tennessee, Alabama—non-union states where wages were low. During the 1980s, many more industries (steel, auto, etc.) closed up shop, moving on to the "more competitive atmospheres" of Mexico, Brazil, or Taiwan where wages were a mere fraction of those in the U.S., and environmental, health and safety standards were much lower. Most seriously hurt by these plant closures and layoffs were African-Americans and other semi-skilled workers in urban centers who lost their decent paying industrial jobs.

Into the gaping economic hole left by the exodus of jobs from U.S. cities has rushed another economy: the drug economy.

THE WAR ON DRUGS

The "War on Drugs," launched by President Reagan in the mid-eighties, has been fought on interlocking international and domestic fronts.

At the international level, the war on drugs has been both a cynical cover-up of U.S. government involvement in the drug trade, as well as justification for U.S. military intervention and control in the Third World.

Over the last 50 years, the primary goal of U.S. foreign policy (and the military industrial complex) has been to fight communism and protect corporate interests. To this end, the U.S. government has, with regularity, formed strategic alliances with drug dealers throughout the world. At the conclusion of World War II, the OSS (precursor to the CIA) allied itself with heroin traders on the docks of Marseille in an effort to wrest power away from communist dock workers. During the Vietnam war, the CIA aided the heroin producing Hmong tribesmen in the Golden Triangle area. In return for cooperation with the U.S. government's war against the Vietcong and other national liberation forces, the CIA flew local heroin out of Southeast Asia and into America. It's no accident that heroin addiction in the U.S. rose exponentially in the 1960s.

Nor is it an accident that cocaine began to proliferate in the United States during the 1980s. Central America is the strategic halfway point for air travel between Colombia and the United States. The Contra War against Sandinista Nicaragua, as well as the war against the national liberation forces in El Salvador, was largely about control of this critical area. When Congress cut off support for the Contras, Oliver North and friends found other ways to fund the Contra re-supply operations, in part through drug dealing. Planes loaded with arms for the Contras took off from the southern United States, offloaded their weapons on private landing strips in Honduras, then loaded up with cocaine for the return trip.

A 1996 exposé by the *San Jose Mercury News* documented CIA involvement in a

Nicaraguan drug ring which poured thousands of kilos of cocaine into Los Angeles' African-American neighborhoods in the 1980s. Drug boss, Danilo Blandon, now an informant for the DEA, acknowledged under oath the drugs-for-weapons deals with the CIA-sponsored Contras.

U.S. military presence in Central and Latin America has not stopped drug traffic. But it has influenced aspects of the drug trade, and is a powerful force of social control in the region. U.S. military intervention—whether in propping up dictators or squashing peasant uprisings—now operates under cover of the righteous war against drugs and "narco-terrorism."

In Mexico, for example, U.S. military aid supposedly earmarked for the drug war is being used to arm Mexican troops in the southern part of the country. The drug trade, however (production, transfer, and distribution points) is all in the north. The "drug war money" is being used primarily to fight against the Zapatista rebels in the southern state of Chiapas who are demanding land reform and economic policy changes which are diametrically opposed to the transnational corporate agenda.

In the Colombian jungles of Cartagena de Chaira, coca has become the only viable commercial crop. In 1996, 30,000 farmers blocked roads and airstrips to prevent crop spraying from aircraft. The Revolutionary Armed Forces of Colombia (FARC) one of the oldest guerrilla organizations in Latin America, held 60 government soldiers hostage for nine months, demanding that the military leave the jungle, that social services be increased, and that alternative crops be made available to farmers. And given the notorious involvement of Colombia's highest officials with the powerful drug cartels, it is not surprising that most U.S. "drug war" military aid actually goes to fighting the guerrillas.

One result of the international war on drugs has been the internationalization of the U.S. prison population. For the most part, it is the low level "mules" carrying drugs into this country who are captured and incarcerated in ever-increasing numbers. At least 25% of inmates in the federal prison system today will be subject to deportation when their sentences are completed.

Here at home, the war on drugs has been a war on poor people. Particularly poor, urban, African-American men and women. It's well documented that police enforcement of the new, harsh drug laws have been focused on low-level dealers in communities of color. Arrests of African-Americans have been about five times higher than arrests of whites, although whites and African-Americans use drugs at about the same rate. And, African-Americans have been imprisoned in numbers even more disproportionate than their relative arrest rates. It is estimated that in 1994, on any given day, one out of every 128

U.S. adults was incarcerated, while one out of every 17 African-American adult males was incarcerated.

The differential in sentencing for powder and crack cocaine is one glaring example of institutionalized racism. About 90% of crack arrests are of African-Americans, while 75% of powder cocaine arrests are of whites. Under federal law, it takes only five grams of crack cocaine to trigger a five-year mandatory minimum sentence. But it takes 500 grams of powder cocaine—100 times as much—to trigger this same sentence. This flagrant injustice was highlighted by a 1996 nationwide federal prison rebellion when Congress refused to enact changes in sentencing laws that would equalize penalties.

Statistics show that police repression and mass incarceration are not curbing the drug trade. Dealers are forced to move, turf is reshuffled, already vulnerable families are broken up. But the demand for drugs still exists, as do huge profits for high-level dealers in this fifty billion dollar international industry.

From one point of view, the war on drugs can actually be seen as a pre-emptive strike. The state's repressive apparatus working overtime. Put poor people away before they get angry. Incarcerate those at the bottom, the helpless, the hopeless, before they demand change. What drugs don't damage (in terms of intact communities, the ability to take action, to organize) the war on drugs and mass imprisonment will surely destroy.

The crackdown on drugs has not stopped drug use. But it has taken thousands of unemployed (and potentially angry and rebellious) young men and women off the streets. And it has created a mushrooming prison population.

PRISON LABOR

An American worker who once upon a time made $8/hour, loses his job when the company relocates to Thailand where workers are paid only $2/day. Unemployed, and alienated from a society indifferent to his needs, he becomes involved in the drug economy or some other outlawed means of survival. He is arrested, put in prison, and put to work. His new salary: 22 cents/hour.

From worker, to unemployed, to criminal, to convict laborer, the cycle has come full circle. And the only victor is big business.

For private business, prison labor is like a pot of gold. No strikes. No union organizing. No unemployment insurance or workers' compensation to pay. No language problem, as in a foreign country. New leviathan prisons are being built with thousands of eerie acres of factories inside the walls. Prisoners do data entry for Chevron, make telephone reservations for TWA, raise hogs, shovel manure, make circuit boards, limousines, water-beds, and lingerie for Victoria's Secret. All at a fraction of the cost of "free labor."

Prisoners can be forced to work for pennies because they have no rights. Even the 14th Amendment to the Constitution which abolished slavery, excludes prisoners from its protections.

And, more and more, prisons are charging inmates for basic necessities—from medical care, to toilet paper, to use of the law library. Many states are now charging "room and board." Berks County jail in Pennsylvania is charging inmates $10 per day to be there. California has similar legislation pending. So, while government cannot (yet) actually require inmates to work at private industry jobs for less than minimum wage, they are forced to by necessity.

Some prison enterprises are state run. Inmates working at UNICOR (the federal prison industry corporation) make recycled furniture and work 40 hours a week for about $40 per month. The Oregon Prison Industries produces a line of "Prison Blues" blue jeans. An ad in their catalogue shows a handsome prison inmate saying, "I say we should make bell-bottoms. They say I've been in here too long." Bizarre, but true. The promotional tags on the clothes themselves actually tout their operation as rehabiliation and job training for prisoners, who of course would never be able to find work in the garment industry upon release.

Prison industries are often directly competing with private industry. Small furniture manufacturers around the country complain that they are being driven out of business by UNICOR which pays 23 cents/hour and has the inside track on government contracts. In another case, U.S. Technologies sold its electronics plant in Austin, Texas, leaving its 150 workers unemployed. Six week later, the electronics plant reopened in a nearby prison.

WELCOME TO THE NEW WORLD ORDER

The proliferation of prisons in the United States is one piece of a puzzle called the globalization of capital.

Since the end of the Cold War, capitalism has gone on an international business offensive. No longer impeded by an alternative socialist economy or the threat of national liberation movements supported by the Soviet Union or China, transnational corporations see the world as their oyster. Agencies such as the World Trade Organization, World Bank, and the International Monetary Fund, bolstered by agreements like NAFTA and GATT are putting more and more power into the hands of transnational corporations by putting the squeeze on national governments. The primary mechanism of control is debt. For decades, developing countries have depended on foreign loans, resulting in increasing vulnerability to the transnational corporate strategy for the global economy. Access to international credit and aid is given only if governments agree to certain conditions known as "structural adjustment."

In a nutshell, structural adjustment requires cuts in social services, privatization of state-run industry, repeal of agreements with labor about working conditions and minimum wage, conversion of multi-use farm lands into cash crop agriculture for export, and the dismantling of trade laws which protect local economies. Under structural adjustment, police and military expenditures are the only government spending that is encouraged. The sovereignty of nations is compromised when, as in the case of Vietnam, trade sanctions are threatened unless the government allows Camel cigarettes to litter the countryside with billboards, or promises to spend millions in the U.S.-orchestrated crackdown on drugs.

The basic transnational corporate philosophy is this: the world is a single market; natural resources are to be exploited; people are consumers; anything which hinders profit is to be routed out and destroyed. The results of this philosophy in action are that while economies are growing, so is poverty, so is ecological destruction, so are sweatshops and child labor. Across the globe, wages are plummeting, indigenous people are being forced off their lands, rivers are becoming industrial dumping grounds, and forests are being obliterated. Massive regional starvation and "World Bank riots" are becoming more frequent throughout the Third World.

All over the world, more and more people are being forced into illegal activity for their own survival as traditional cultures and social structures are destroyed. Inevitably, crime and imprisonment rates are on the rise. And the United States law enforcement establishment is in the forefront, domestically and internationally, in providing state-of-the-art repression.

Within the United States, structural adjustment (sometimes known as the Contract With America) takes the form of welfare and social service cuts, continued massive military spending, and skyrocketing prison spending. Walk through any poor urban neighborhood: school systems are crumbling, after-school programs, libraries, parks and drug treatment centers are closed. But you will see more police stations and more cops. Often, the only "social service" available to poor young people is jail.

The dismantling of social programs, and the growing dominance of the right-wing agenda in U.S. politics has been made possible, at least in part, by the successful repression of the civil rights and liberation movements of the 1960s and 70s. Many of the leaders—Martin Luther King Jr., Malcolm X, Fred Hampton, and many others—were assassinated. Others, like Geronimo ji Jaga Pratt, Leonard Peltier, and Mumia Abu-Jamal, have been locked up. Over 150 political leaders from the black liberation struggle, the Puerto Rican independence movement, and other resistance efforts are still in prison. Many are serving sentences ranging from 40 to 90 years. Oppressed communities have been robbed of radical political leadership which might have led an opposition movement. We are reaping the results.

The number of people in U.S. prisons has more than tripled in the past 17 years—from 500,000 in 1980 to 1.8 million in 1997. Today, more than five million people are behind bars, on parole, probation, or under other supervision by the criminal justice system. The state of California now spends more on prisons than on higher education, and over the past decade has built 19 prisons and only one branch university.

Add to this, the fact that increasing numbers of women are being locked up. Between 1980 and 1994, the number of women in prison increased five-fold, and women now make up the fastest growing segment of the prison population. Most of these women are mothers—leaving future generations growing up in foster homes or on the streets.

Welcome to the New World Order.

WHAT IS TO BE DONE

Prisons are not reducing crime. But they are fracturing already vulnerable families and communities.

Poor people of color are being locked up in grossly disproportionate numbers, primarily for nonviolent crimes. But Americans are not feeling safer.

As "criminals" become scapegoats for our floundering economy and our deteriorating social structure, even the guise of rehabilitation is quickly disappearing from our penal philosophy. After all: rehabilitate for what? To go back into an economy which has no jobs? To go back into a community which has no hope? As education and other prison programs are cut back, or in most cases eliminated altogether, prisons are becoming vast, overcrowded, holding tanks. Or worse: factories behind bars.

And, prison labor is undercutting wages—something which hurts all working and poor Americans. It's a situation which can only occur because organized labor is divided and weak and has not kept step with organized capital.

While capital has globalized, labor has not. While the transnationals truly are fashioning our planet into a global village, there is still little communication or cooperation between workers around the world. Only an internationally linked labor movement can effectively challenge the power of the transnational corporations.

There have been some wonderful, shining instances of international worker solidarity. In the early 1980s, 3M workers in South Africa walked out in support of striking 3M workers in New Jersey. Recently, longshore workers in Denmark, Spain, Sweden and several other countries closed down ports around the world in solidarity with striking Liverpool dockers. The company was forced to negotiate. When Renault closed its plant in Belgium, 100,000 demonstrated in Brussels, pressuring the French and Belgium governments to condemn the plant closure and compel its reopening.

Here in the U.S., there is a glimmer of hope as the AFL-CIO has voted in some new, more progressive leadership. We'll see how that shapes up, and whether the last 50 years of anti-communist, bread-and-butter American unionism is really a thing of the past.

What is certain is that resistance to the transnational corporate agenda is growing around the globe:

- In 1996, the people of Bougainville, a small New Guinea island, organized a secessionist rebellion, protesting the dislocations and ecological destruction caused by corporate mining on the island. When the government hired mercenaries from South Africa to train local troops in counterinsurgency warfare, the army rebelled, threw out the mercenaries, and deposed the Prime Minister.

- A one day General Strike shut down Haiti in January 1997. Strikers demanded the suspension of negotiations between the Prime Minister and the International Monetary Fund/World Bank. They protested the austerity measures imposed by the IMF and WB which would mean laying off 7,000 government workers and the privatization of the electric and telephone companies.

- In Nigeria, the Ogoni people conducted a protracted eight year struggle against Shell Oil. Acid rain, and hundreds of oil spills and gas flares were turning the once fertile countryside into a near wasteland. Their peaceful demonstrations, election boycotts, and pleas for international solidarity were met with violent government repression and the eventual execution of Ogoni writer-leader Ken Saro Wiwa.

- In France, a month-long General Strike united millions of workers who protested privatization, a government worker pay freeze, and cutbacks in social services. Telephone, airline, power, postal, education, health care and metal workers all joined together, bringing business to a standstill. The right-wing Chirac government was forced to make minor concessions before being voted out for a new "socialist" administration.

- At the Oak Park Heights Correctional Facility in Minnesota, 150 prisoners went on strike in March 1997, demanding to be paid the minimum wage. Although they lost a litigation battle to attain this right, their strike gained attention and support from several local labor unions.

Just as the prison-industrial complex is becoming increasingly central to the growth of the U.S. economy, prisoners are a crucial part of building effective opposition to the transnational corporate agenda. Because of their enforced invisibility, powerlessness, and isolation, it's far too common for prisoners to be left out of the equation of international solidarity. Yet, opposing the expansion of the prison-industrial complex, and supporting the rights and basic humanity of prisoners, may be the only way we can stave off the consolidation of a police state that represses us all—where you or a friend or family member may end up behind bars.

Clearly, the only alternative that will match the power of global capital is an internationalization of human solidarity. Because, truly, we are all in this together.

"International solidarity is not an act of charity. It is an act of unity between allies fighting on different terrains toward the same objective. The foremost of these objectives is to aid the development of humanity to the highest level possible."

—Samora Machel (1933-1986)
Leader of FRELIMO
First President of Mozambique

REFERENCES

Books:

Burton-Rose, Daniel, Dan Pens and Paul Wright (eds) *The Celling of America: An Inside Look at the US Prison Industry*, Common Courage Press, 1998.

Donziger, Stephen R. (ed), *The Real War on Crime*, Harper Perennial, 1996.

Rosenblatt, Elihu (ed), *Criminal Injustice*, South End Press, 1996.

Print Articles:

"A Matter of Fact," *Prison Legal News*, Dec. 1996.

"Another Face of Neo-Liberalism: Drug Trafficking and Commercial Banks," *Bulldozer*. Reprinted from "Report on Canada's Sixth Year in the OAS: Focus on Corruption," *Canada-Americas Policy Alternatives.*

Bernstein, Dennis and Leslie Kean, "People of the Opiate," *The Nation*, Dec. 16, 1996.

"Coca Clashes: Colombia," *The Economist*, Aug. 17, 1996.

Cooper, Marc, "Labor Deals a New Hand," *The Nation*, March 24, 1997.

Day, Christopher, "Neoliberalism and World Revolution," *Love and Rage*, Mar/Apr. 1997.

Dunkel, G., "General Strike Shuts Haiti for a Day," *Workers World*, Jan. 30, 1997.

REFERENCES

Dunne, Bill, "The New Plantation," *Prison Legal News*, Feb. 1997.

"Furniture Manufacturers Threatened by UNICOR," *Prison Legal News*, July 1996.

Gillenkirk, Jeff and Brian Wilson, "Mexican Unrest: The 80s Parallels," *San Franciscio Chronicle*, June 10, 1997.

"Latin America's Other Hostages," *The Economist*, Jan. 25 1997.

"Leftist Colombian Rebels Free 70 Troops After Army Pullback," Chronicle News Services, *San Francscio Chronicle*, June 16, 1997.

"Minnesota Prisoners Strike for Minimum Wage," *Prison Legal News*, July 1996. Reprinted from *Workers World*, March 21, 1996.

Mollins, Carl "Prisons for Profit," *Maclean's*, June 5, 1995.

Parenti, Christian, "Inside Jobs," *New Statesman*, Nov. 3, 1995.

Parenti, Christian, "Making Prisons Pay," *The Nation*, Jan. 29 1996.

Parenti, Christian, "Pay Now, Pay Later," *The Progressive*, July 26, 1996.

"Second Circuit Rejects Prison FLSA Claim, Modifies Standard," *Prison Legal News*, Jan. 1997.

"Standing guard for Uncle Sam: Colombia," *The Economist*, Jan. 14, 1995.

Webb, Gary and Pamela Kramer, "Drug Dealer Told of Relationship with CIA," *Knight-Ridder/Tribune News Service*, Oct. 5, 1996.

Wisely, Willie, "The Bottom Line: California's Prison Industry Authority," *Out of Time*, Feb. 1996.

Internet Articles:

Dropkin, Greg, "Worldwide Action in Support of Mersey," LaborNet Report.

Haq, Farhan, "U.S.-Vietnam: McDonald's 'Happy Meals' Make Workers Sad," Inner Press Service.

Lowry, Suzanne, "French Strikers Win First Round," LaborNet Report.

Tran, Dr. Ho, and Mark Takano, "Just Don't Do It: Say No to Labor Exploitation," Open Letter, Nov. 18, 1996.

Resource List

Anarchist Black Cross Federation
NJ ABC-BG
PO Box 8532
Patterson, NJ 07508-8532
http://burn.ucsd.edu/~abcf

California Prison Focus & H.I.P. (HIV In Prison)
2940 16th St. #307
San Francisco, CA 94103
www.prisons.org

Coalition for Prisoner Rights
Box 1911
Santa Fe, NM 87504

Critical Resistance East
460 W. 128 St.
New York, NY 10027
Phone: 917.493.9795
Fax: 917.493.9798
crne@criticalresistance.org
www.criticalresistance.org

The Fire Inside
c/o California Coalition for Women Prisoners
1540 Market St. #490
San Francisco, CA 94102

Libertad
2607 W. Division
Chicago, IL 60622
Libertad carries news and information from the National Committee to Free Puerto Rican Prisoners of War.

Out of Time
3542 18th St. Box 30
San Francisco, CA 94110
Newsletter of the Out of Control Lesbian Committee to Support Women Political Prisoners and Prisoners of War.

Prison Activist Resource Center
BOX 339
Berkeley, CA 94701
Tel: 510-893-4648
Fax: 510-893-4607
parc@prisonactivist.org
www.prisonactivist.org

Prison Art Newsletter
PO Box 31574
San Francisco, CA 94131
info@prisonart.org

Prison Legal News
2400 NW 80th St. #148
Seattle, WA 98117
www.prisonlegalnews.org

RAZE the WALLS
Box 720418
Orlando, FL 32872
Provides prisoner support and abolition work.

This Just In
103 Bartlett Ave.
Pittsfield, MA 01201

Transformation
c/o Women's Project
2224 Main St.
Little Rock, AR 72206
A quarterly newsletter for social and economic justice by groups working with women prisoners since 1989.

Walking Steel/Can't Jail the Spirit
Box 578172
Chicago, IL 60657
CEML@aol.com
Walking Steel carries written materials including a collection of bios on some of the current political prisoners in the U.S.

EVE GOLDBERG is a writer, filmmaker, and prisoners' rights activist.

LINDA EVANS is a former anti-imperialist political prisoner. She was incarcerated at the Federal Correctional Institute in Dublin, California for 16 years. Linda was released in 2001 via a pardon by president Bill Clinton, along with Susan Rosenberg, another political prisoner.

Linda and Eve currently live in Santa Rosa, California.

ABOUT PM PRESS

PM Press was founded at the end of 2007 by a small collection of folks with decades of publishing, media, and organizing experience. We seek to create radical and stimulating fiction and non-fiction books, pamphlets, t-shirts, visual and audio materials to entertain, educate and inspire you. We aim to distribute these through every available channel with every available technology—whether that means you are seeing anarchist classics at our bookfair stalls; reading our latest vegan cookbook at the café; downloading geeky fiction e-books; or digging new music and timely videos from our website.

PM Press is always on the lookout for talented and skilled volunteers, artists, activists and writers to work with. If you have a great idea for a project or can contribute in some way, please get in touch.

PM Press . PO Box 23912 . Oakland CA 94623 . www.pmpress.org